MINI FAKE BOOK FOR CLARINET

101 favourite songs and melodies
101 beliebte Songs und Melodien
101 chansons et mélodies à succès

Arranged by Sally Adams with Paul Harris

FABER *ff* MUSIC

The text paper used in this publication is a virgin fibre product that is manufactured in the UK to ISO 14001 standards. The wood fibre used is only sourced from managed forests using sustainable forestry principles. This paper is 100% recyclable.

ISBN 0-571-52686-1
EAN 978-0-571-52686-4

© 2008 by Faber Music Ltd
First published in 2008 by Faber Music Ltd
3 Queen Square London WC1N 3AU

Cover by Lydia Merrills-Ashcroft
Music processed by Jackie Leigh

Printed in England by Caligraving Ltd

To buy Faber Music publications or to find out about the full range of titles available please contact your local retailer or Faber Music sales enquiries:

Faber Music Limited, Burnt Mill,
Elizabeth Way, Harlow CM20 2HX England
Tel: +44 (0) 1279 82 89 82
Fax: +44 (0) 1279 82 89 83
sales@fabermusic.com fabermusic.com

CONTENTS

FOREWORD

Before you begin playing the pieces in this book, prepare them carefully. Here's a good way to start work on each piece:

1. Think about the key and then play the scale (or the micro-scale, which is just the first five notes).
2. Then make sure you really understand the rhythm: clap the rhythm while tapping the pulse with your foot, for example.
3. Then explore the piece's 'ingredients' – articulation (e.g. staccato and accents) and dynamic markings. Play the scale again adding some of these markings or perhaps make up your own short piece that uses these same ingredients.
4. Finally think about the character or mood. How will you really bring the piece to life and convey its personality?

Above all enjoy your performances and always play with real musicianship and energy!

A NOTE ON CHORD SYMBOLS
Chord symbols have been included here in the key of the instrument. However, a separate PDF of chord symbols at concert pitch (for piano accompanying purposes) can be downloaded from fabermusic.com.

(MEET) THE FLINTSTONES

Words and Music by Joseph Barbera,
William Hanna and Hoyt Curtin

WHEN A KNIGHT WON HIS SPURS

Trad.

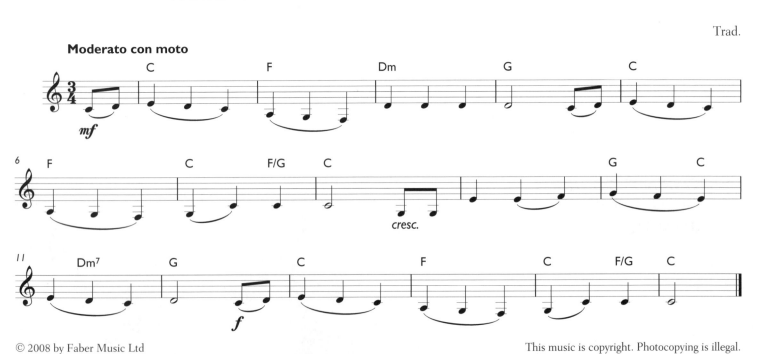

THEME FROM SYMPHONY No.1

Johannes Brahms

I TAUT I TAW A PUDDY-TAT

Words and Music by Billy May,
Warren Foster and Alan Livingston

MORNING MISTS

Paul Harris

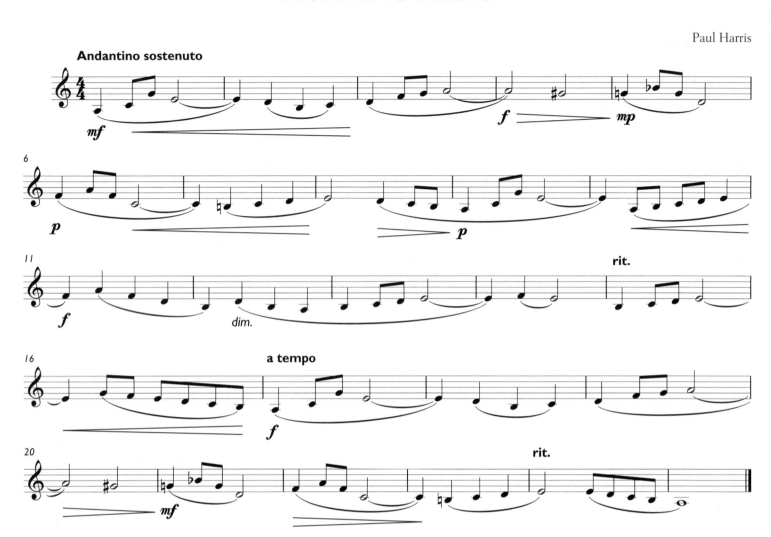

LITTLE DONKEY

Words and Music by
Eric Boswell

SLANE

Trad. Irish

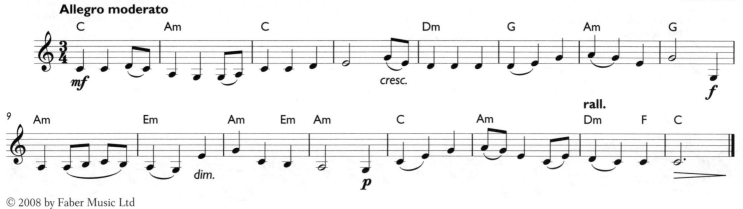

TRULY SCRUMPTIOUS
(FROM *CHITTY CHITTY BANG BANG*)

Words and Music by
Richard Sherman and Robert Sherman

PROMENADE
(FROM *PICTURES AT AN EXHIBITION*)

Modest Musorgsky

AUSTRIAN HYMN

Joseph Haydn

NEW KILLARNEY POLKA

Trad.

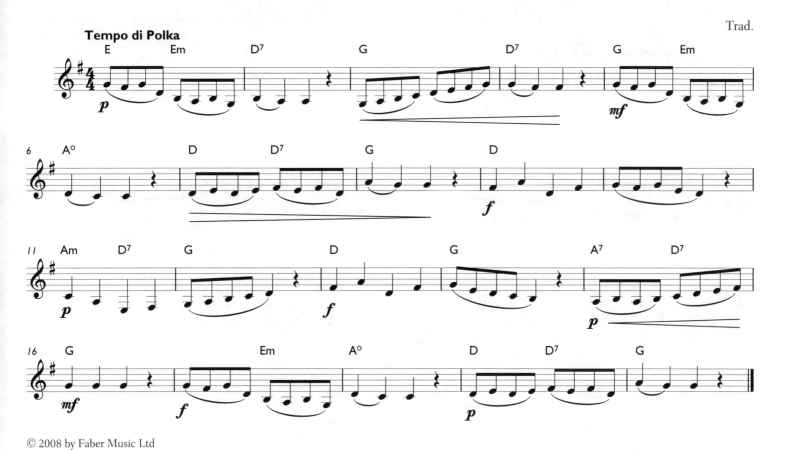

BEAUTIFUL DREAMER

Stephen Foster

18.5.14

TOP CAT

Words and Music by William Hanna,
Joseph Barbera and Hoyt Curtin

HYFRYDOL

R. H. Prichard

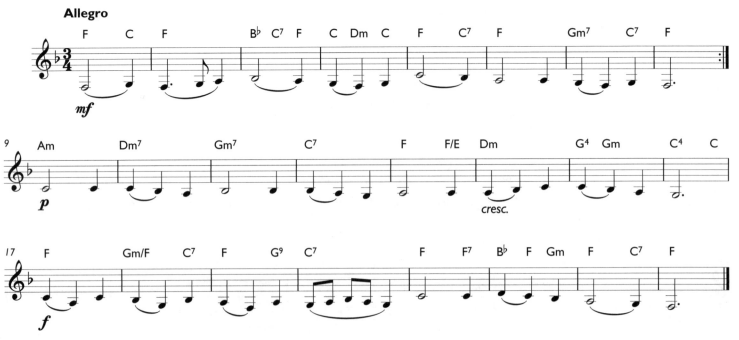

THE HIPPOPOTAMUS

Words by Michael Flanders
Music by Donald Swann

THE ROSE OF TRALEE

Charles W. Glover

SUNRISE, SUNSET
(FROM *FIDDLER ON THE ROOF*)

Words by Sheldon Harnick
Music by Jerry Bock

THE COONEY TUNE BLUES
(*for Joseph Cooney*)

Sally Adams

CABARET
(FROM *CABARET*)

Words by Fred Ebb
Music by John Kander

CHITTY CHITTY BANG BANG
(FROM *CHITTY CHITTY BANG BANG*)

Words and Music by
Richard Sherman and Robert Sherman

DON'T FENCE ME IN
(FROM *HOLLYWOOD CANTEEN*)

Words and Music by
Cole Porter

DANCE OF THE HOURS
(FROM *LA GIOCONDA*)

Amilcare Ponchielli

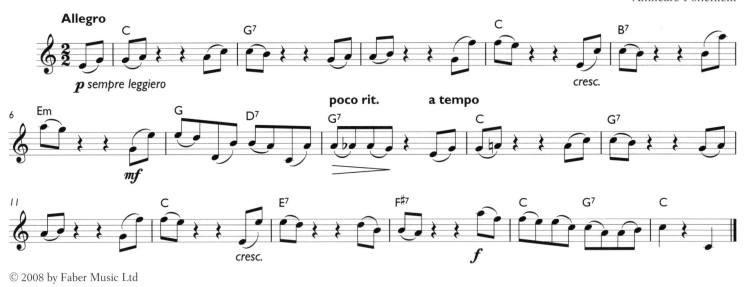

THE BARE NECESSITIES
(FROM *THE JUNGLE BOOK*)

Words and Music by
Terry Gilkyson

FROSTY THE SNOWMAN

Words and Music by
Steve Nelson and Jack Rollins

MAYPOLE DANCE

Paul Harris

2.7.15

LET'S CALL THE WHOLE THING OFF
(FROM *SHALL WE DANCE?*)

Lively, with a bounce, for 22.10.15

Words and Music by
George Gershwin and Ira Gershwin

DANSE DES MIRLITONS
(FROM *THE NUTCRACKER*)

Pyotr Ilyich Tchaikovsky

Moderato sempre leggiero

WHEN YOU WISH UPON A STAR
(FROM *PINOCCHIO*)

Words by Ned Washington
Music by Leigh Harline

With expression

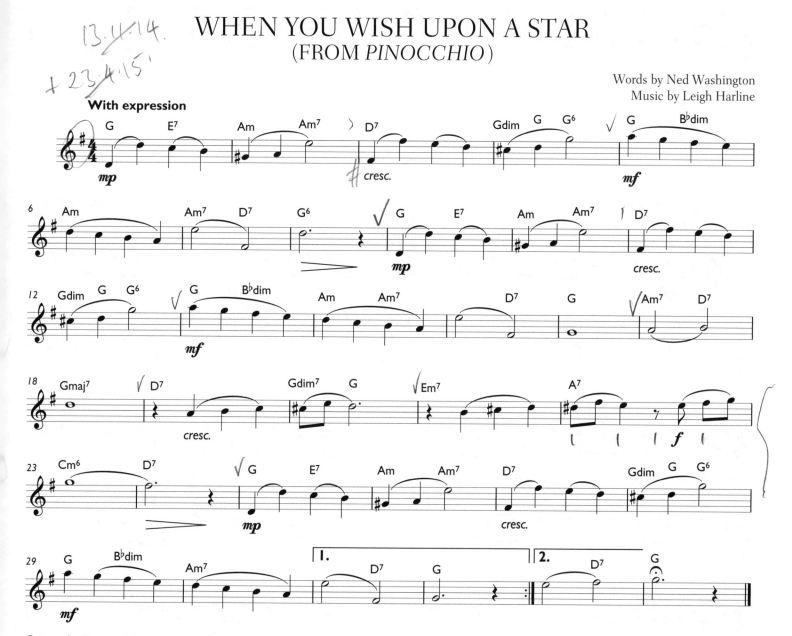

AGINCOURT SONG

Anon.

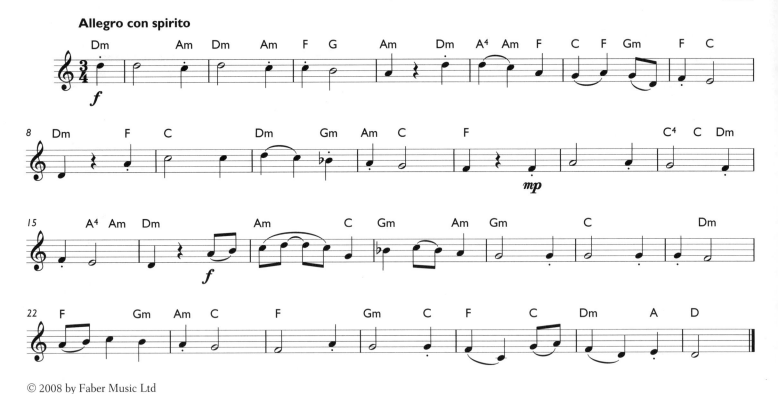

COME YE SONS OF ART

Henry Purcell

CAN'T GET YOU OUT OF MY HEAD

Words and Music by
Cathy Dennis and Robert Davis

JERUSALEM

Charles Hubert Hastings Parry

A SPOONFUL OF SUGAR
(FROM *MARY POPPINS*)

Words and Music by
Richard Sherman and Robert Sherman

MAKE ME SMILE (COME UP AND SEE ME)

Words and Music by
Steve Harley

RULE BRITANNIA!

Thomas Augustine Arne

LIKE A PRAYER

Words and Music by
Madonna and Pat Leonard

WAIT FOR THE WAGGON

Trad.

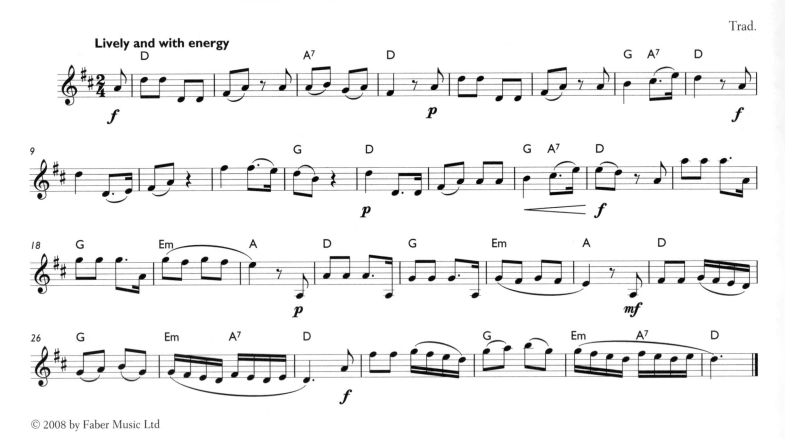

SOMEBODY LOVES ME
(FROM *GEORGE WHITE'S SCANDALS OF 1924*)

Words by Buddy De Sylva and Ballard MacDonald
Music by George Gershwin

BOURBONS

Sally Adams

IF I WERE A RICH MAN
(FROM *FIDDLER ON THE ROOF*)

Words by Sheldon Harnick
Music by Jerry Bock

ROCKIN' ROBIN

Words and Music by
Jimmie Thomas

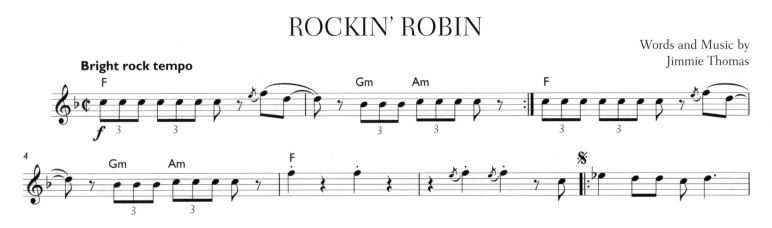

BLOW, BLOW, THOU WINTER WIND

Thomas Augustine Arne

ZIP-A-DEE-DOO-DAH
(FROM *SONG OF THE SOUTH*)

Words by Ray Gilbert
Music by Allie Wrubel

FLY ME TO THE MOON (IN OTHER WORDS)

Words and Music by
Bart Howard

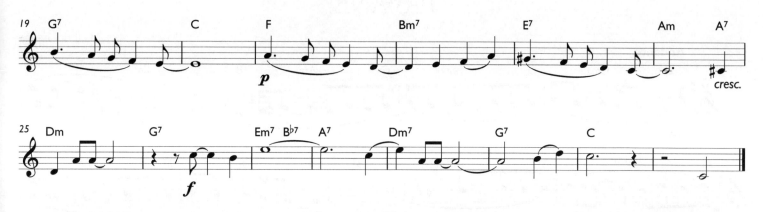

TIPSY TANGO

Paul Harris

PAVANE

Gabriel Fauré

GET ME TO THE CHURCH ON TIME
(FROM *MY FAIR LADY*)

Words by Alan Jay Lerner
Music by Frederick Loewe

14.7.16

TOMORROW
(FROM *ANNIE*)

Words by Martin Charnin
Music by Charles Strouse

AVE VERUM CORPUS

Wolfgang Amadeus Mozart

© 2008 by Faber Music Ltd

ETUDE Op.10 No.3

Frédéric Chopin

© 2008 by Faber Music Ltd

(SITTIN' ON) THE DOCK OF THE BAY

Words and Music by
Otis Redding and Steve Cropper

A WHITER SHADE OF PALE

Words and Music by
Keith Reid and Gary Brooker

BYRNES HORNPIPE

Trad.

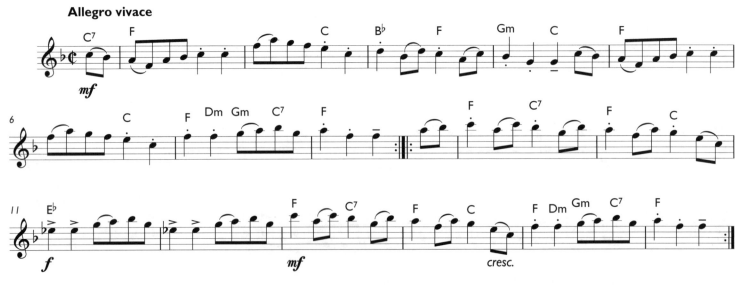

PIE JESU
(FROM THE REQUIEM)

Gabriel Fauré

THE PRINCE OF DENMARK'S MARCH

Jeremiah Clarke

(IS THIS THE WAY TO) AMARILLO?

Words and Music by
Neil Sedaka and Howard Greenfield

SICILIENNE FOR SALLY

Paul Harris

ANDANTE
(FROM THE VIOLIN CONCERTO)

Felix Mendelssohn

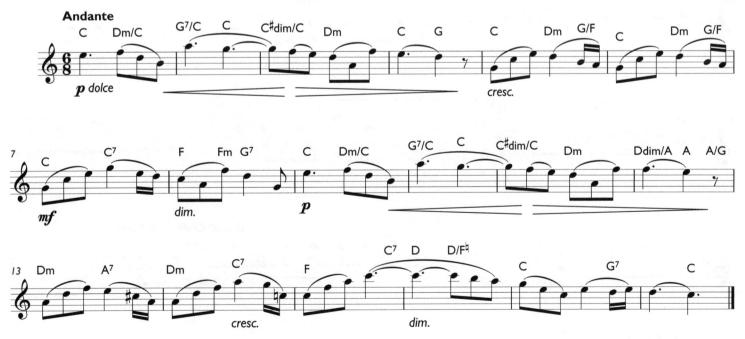

KILLING ME SOFTLY WITH HIS SONG

Words by Norman Gimbel
Music by Charles Fox

HEDWIG'S THEME
(FROM *HARRY POTTER AND THE PHILOSOPHER'S STONE*)

Music by John Williams

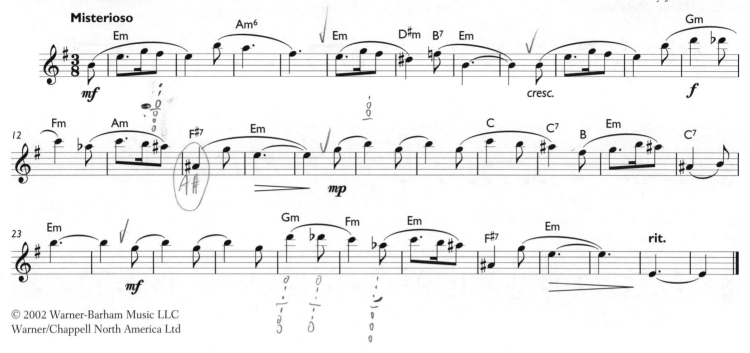

THE FLOWERS THAT BLOOM IN THE SPRING
(FROM *THE MIKADO*)

W. S. Gilbert & Arthur Sullivan

LULLABY OF BROADWAY

Words by Al Dubin
Music by Harry Warren

WHO WANTS TO BE A MILLIONAIRE?
(FROM *HIGH SOCIETY*)

Words and Music by
Cole Porter

LA DONNA È MOBILE
(FROM *RIGOLETTO*)

Giuseppe Verdi

YOU'RE BEAUTIFUL

Words and Music by James Blunt,
Sacha Skarbek and Amanda Ghost

THE CAN-CAN
(FROM *ORPHEUS IN THE UNDERWORLD*)

Jacques Offenbach

VOCALISE

Sally Adams

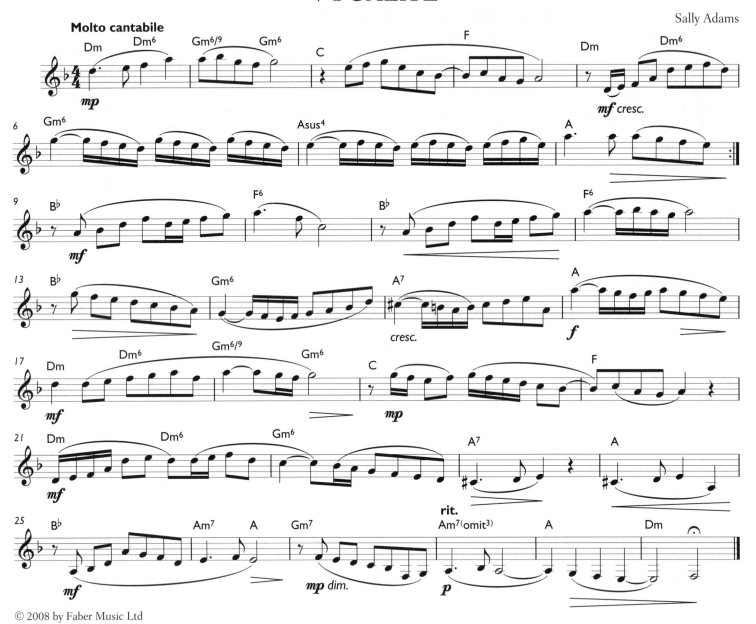

ANYTHING GOES
(FROM *ANYTHING GOES*)

Words and Music by
Cole Porter

THEME
(FROM *SWAN LAKE*)

Pyotr Ilyich Tchaikovsky

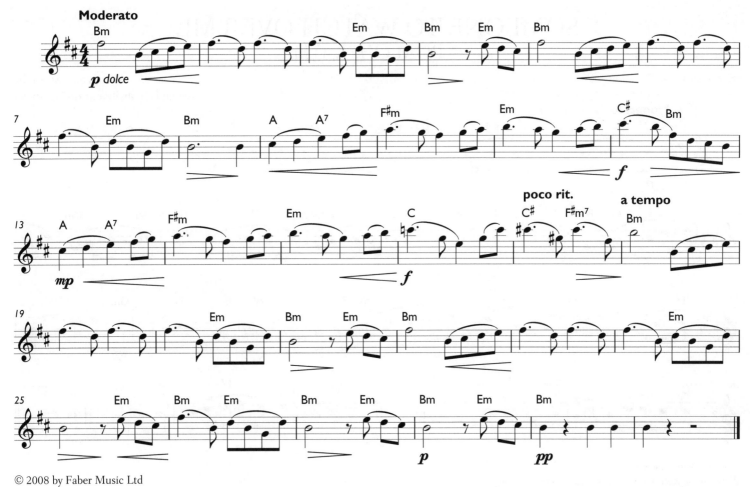

SPRING SONG

Felix Mendelssohn

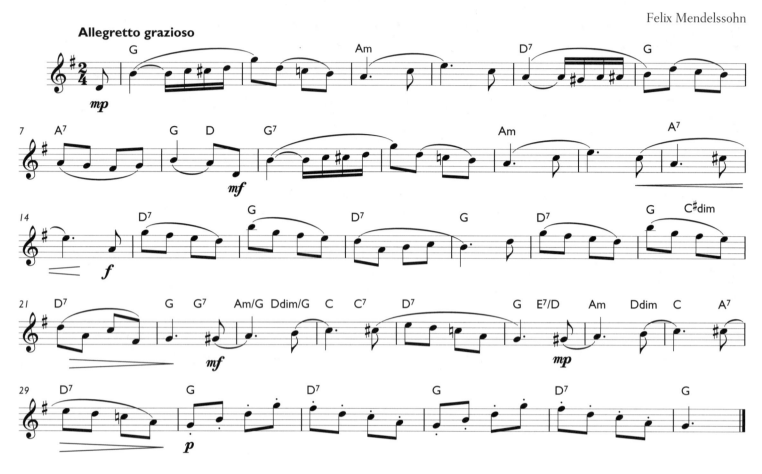

SOMEONE TO WATCH OVER ME
(FROM *OH, KAY!*)

Words and Music by
George Gershwin and Ira Gershwin

AVE MARIA

Franz Schubert

NYMPHS AND SHEPHERDS

Henry Purcell

DIXIE

Daniel Emmett

MISS OTIS REGRETS (SHE'S UNABLE TO LUNCH TODAY)
(FROM *HI DIDDLE DIDDLE*)

Words and Music by
Cole Porter

WAKE ME UP BEFORE YOU GO-GO

Words and Music by
George Michael

POLOVTSIAN DANCE
(FROM *PRINCE IGOR*)

Alexander Borodin

THE SUN WHOSE RAYS ARE ALL ABLAZE
(FROM *THE MIKADO*)

W. S. Gilbert & Arthur Sullivan

BACK FOR GOOD

Words and Music by
Gary Barlow

WINTER
(FROM *THE SEASONS*)

Antonio Vivaldi

PLAISIR D'AMOUR

Johann Paul Martini

SUMMER NIGHTS
(FROM *GREASE*)

Words and Music by
Jim Jacobs and Warren Casey

THE MAN WITH THE CHILD IN HIS EYES

Words and Music by
Kate Bush

SONG OF INDIA
(FROM *SADKO*)

Nicholas Rimsky-Korsakoff

ANGELS

Words and Music by
Robert Williams and Guy Chambers

WOULDN'T IT BE LOVERLY?
(FROM *MY FAIR LADY*)

Words by Alan Jay Lerner
Music by Frederick Loewe

IN THE HALL OF THE MOUNTAIN KING
(FROM *PEER GYNT*)

Edvard Grieg

I'M A BELIEVER

Words and Music by
Neil Diamond

THEME FROM THE *NEW WORLD* SYMPHONY

Antonin Dvořák

TRÄUMEREI

Robert Schumann

WE GO TOGETHER
(FROM *GREASE*)

Words and Music by
Jim Jacobs and Warren Casey

THE SWAN
(FROM *THE CARNIVAL OF THE ANIMALS*)

Camille Saint-Saëns

DANCING QUEEN

Words and Music by Stig Anderson,
Benny Andersson and Björn Ulvaeus

ROAD TO NOWHERE

Words and Music by
David Byrne

ABI'S ARIA

Sally Adams

THEME FROM PIANO CONCERTO No.21

Wolfgang Amadeus Mozart

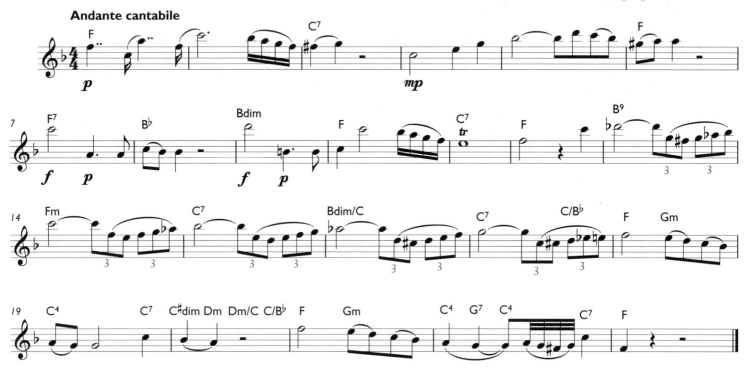

THEME FROM *WILLIAM TELL* OVERTURE

Gioacchino Rossini

IF YOU'RE ANXIOUS FOR TO SHINE
(FROM *PATIENCE*)

W. S. Gilbert & Arthur Sullivan

AIR ON THE G STRING
(FROM SUITE No.3)

Johann Sebastian Bach

THIS TOWN AIN'T BIG ENOUGH
FOR BOTH OF US

Words and Music by
Ronald Mael

GRAND FANTASIA

Paul Harris